ALINE L MOHR

BEHIND CLOSED DOORS

BEHIND CLOSED DOORS

First Printing, 2025

To my husband and best friend Jim,
our four sons and all those living with
eating disorders.

Acknowledgments

I want to express special gratitude to Kim Suhr
for her guidance from the outset. Also, thanks
to the writers in my Wednesday evening roundtable without
whom this never would have been completed.
Finally, thanks to Jim for his encouragement and endless
technical skills.

CHAPTER

1

TWELVE PERSPECTIVES OF RECOGNIZING AN EATING DISORDER:

1. From the mother who hears water running in the bathroom and the daughter vomiting after dinner
2. From the father who watches her push chicken, cut into miniscule morsels, around the plate
3. From the best friend who invites her to lunch and is told, "not lunch, just coffee"
4. From the son who observes she rarely sits down to eat with the family
5. From the neighbor who suggests dinner at a restaurant but notes she always orders a salad
6. From herself looking in the mirror and seeing hollow cheeks and thinning hair
7. From the co-worker who jokes about her thinness saying she must run around in the shower to get wet
8. From the husband who takes note that her clothes bag in the butt
9. From herself seeing only wrinkled skin and loss of muscle when doing yoga

10. From the golfing partner who recognizes her driving distance slips from 150 to 100 yards
11. From the staff at the gym who observe her working out for two hours daily
12. From the sunbathers on the beach who watch a woman walk along the shore clad in a long sleeve shirt

CHAPTER 2

Brown leaves accumulated against the building. My fingers felt numb after the walk from the parking lot. I hesitated then took one last breath of cold air. Time to do it.

I pressed the doorbell alongside the metal door. A buzz. A click sounded. I pulled the door open and walked into a well-lighted hallway. A woman at the opposite end waved me forward. I noticed all the doors along the way were closed. The place resembled a college dorm but did not have the feel of one. Too antiseptic.

"And, would you be Aline?" asked the woman who I guessed to be in her fifties, close to my age. She forced a smile and held a clipboard near her chest.

"Yes, I'm Aline. My therapist told me to come when I sat in her office yesterday. Actually, it was more like a threat: either come in or she wouldn't see me any longer. So here I am." I'd doubted whether the therapist would drop me. I needed the antidepressants she prescribed. But I didn't want to gamble.

"The orders arrived here at Aurora early this morning. Hope you didn't have too much trouble parking. The lot frees up some when the groups let out from the other units around ten o'clock. From now on, you'll be arriving at 10:30, so it shouldn't be a problem."

I wondered, if the parking lot filled, could I turn around and go home?

"What I need from you now is your blood pressure, temperature, and a signature on several forms acknowledging that you're here for treatment of your own volition. Insurance can be tricky, and everything must be signed. Here, take this clipboard and pen, and I'll get your temperature and blood pressure."

I sat down on one of the two chairs across from the nurses' station. Several young people sat in a circle in a large glassed-in room behind me. I began to read over the papers. *Here of my own volition.* No, but I couldn't say that this wasn't my choice, or I'd be screwed. The nurse checked my vitals. "One more thing, Aline. We get a weight taken on everyone at least three times a week. Follow me and I'll get yours."

I set the clipboard down and followed her into a laundry room. Detergent odors filled the small space where a digital scale stood. "Empty your pockets, take off your jacket and shoes and step onto the scale backwards," said the woman who's name tag read *Sharon.*

"Backwards? I have a good idea what I weigh. What difference does it make if I see it?"

"From now on we will keep track of your weight here at the hospital. You will be told by staff not to weigh yourself at home since you're outpatient. The patients here don't know their weight either. The focus is not on a number but recovery."

Right, but I always looked around considering who was the skinniest around me. Numbers were important.

I repocketed my car keys and iPhone then followed Sharon back to the front desk. She looked at the clock on the wall, pointed to the room behind me and said, "Kathryn is teaching about nutrition. They began thirty minutes ago but we won't break for lunch until 12:25 PM, so I'll let you into the group." She opened the door to a room full of girls, plus one guy. Several patients huddled beneath blankets while others colored in Mandala coloring books. “Kathryn, sorry to interrupt but want you to meet Aline. She just checked in and is ready to join the group.”

No, I wasn’t. I wasn’t ready to join any group for discussion about nutrition, and especially with a bunch of teenage girls. Heck, I was a wife and mother of four boys. I knew plenty about feeding swimmers and energy needs. I was fifty-eight years old.

Kathryn directed me to an empty chair next to her. “Welcome. How about you tell us why you’re here, and we will go around the room and introduce ourselves. I’m certain you won’t remember names, but it’s a start.”

“Sure, well, I’m Aline. I’m here because my doctor and therapist said I had to come. I don’t eat a lot.” I didn’t say the word *anorexic.*

“Okay,” said Kathryn. “Tracy, you lead off.”

“Hi, I’m Tracy and I restrict.” She didn’t use the word *anorexic* either.

The girls went around the room quickly and stated first names and whether they were *anorexic* or *bulimic.* Their names didn’t stick with me, but I observed who was looking severely starved. It wasn’t as easy to detect the bulimics. Jack, I’d remember his name since he was the only guy, said he was both anorexic *and* bulimic. I didn’t realize one could be both at the same time.

“Thanks, everyone. Aline, we’ve been talking about the idea of *good and bad* foods; how people tend to look at food as being good for you or bad for you. Problems arise when eating disorder patients believe foods are bad simply because they’re high in calories and should be avoided. That kind of thinking excludes something like avocados which are high in calories but contain lots of nutrients.”

She went on and talked about other misconceptions people held about foods. Pizza was actually healthy because of the carbohydrates, needed for energy, in the crust and the protein in the cheese and meats.

My attention wandered, as I looked around the room and tried to remember names but could only make associations as to who was anorexic and bulimic. Who was thinner than I was. It felt competitive.

"Did everyone turn in their meal plans for the week? If not, I'll take them now. Aline, I'll need to meet with you after lunch and go over what you'll do every day," said Kathryn. "Okay, wash hands and line up for lunch. You inpatients can go back to your rooms to avoid the line for the bathroom."

Everyone pushed aside their blankets, chairs, papers, colored pencils, and books and stood to either return to their rooms off the hall or got in line for the bathroom located in the art room. Kathryn approached me, "Aline, I selected a lunch for you today. The kitchen staff knows you're coming."

Hurray, I thought to myself.

The inpatients reconvened by the nurses' desk. No one seemed to be in a hurry, except for Kathryn and another staff person who introduced herself as *Diane*. Soft spoken for a large woman, she seemed kind and patient with the group. Two student interns also introduced themselves to me, *Katy* and *Elyse*. They were so young, couldn't be much older than the patients. Diane looked over the group, "Is everyone here? No, I see Rachael coming. Okay, let's go." The door buzzed, then clicked after Sharon got a nod from Diane. We all walked out of the unit. I noted two exits out of this section of the hospital. Both required a key or touch pad of some sort.

One of the girls walked alongside me. "You probably don't remember, but I'm Grace. The first day is pretty crazy in here. You end up meeting with the doctor, the intake and insurance people, and anyone else they think of. Tomorrow will be better. Since you're outpatient, you'll be glad to know three other girls are, too, this week. I'm inpatient. Have been for about ten days. I am so ready to get out of here."

I wondered why she was so anxious to leave: rules, loss of freedom, food, staff? I knew I didn't want to be here, but then I didn't look sickly like some of the rest of the patients.

We walked down one hall past a security office, an intake office, and two vending machines with bags of Doritos and Fritos, large candy bars, peanut butter cracker packs and cans of Coke and Mountain Dew. We turned down another hall before we entered a large, well-lighted, crowded cafeteria. The shouts and chatter drowned out our conversation. My panic level rose. The odors from the hot foods made me feel sick to my stomach.

We formed a single line to pick up metal utensils and paper napkins. I followed Grace who grabbed a milk carton and piece of heavily frosted chocolate cake from a refrigerated section. The cake screamed 400 calories, and I couldn't fathom eating it. One of the student interns handed an empty tray to each patient. I noticed a slip of paper on each one. Grace proceeded to get in line to get her plate of food. The intern handed me a tray and instructed me to grab a blue carton of 2% milk and show the servers my menu which lay on my tray. Two-percent milk equaled 120 calories. How many calories would I consume?

I set the milk on the tray, followed Grace in line, and handed the paper to a young woman server who introduced herself as *Ella.* "Is this your first day?"

I nodded.

"Thought so by looking at your menu. Here's the turkey and cheese sandwich. The mayo is around the corner, and here's an apple."

I took the food items, placed them on the tray, and looked around for the mayo. I didn't want mayonnaise. I didn't want a slice of cheese. The crowd had dispersed, so I followed Grace to one of the now empty tables. As she looked over her shoulder, she said, "Our unit eats together, so staff can watch us, make certain we eat everything. Just sit down here next to me. "Hi, Jack. Here we are again, same old, same old."

Seriously, did the staff actually watch us eat?

"Yeah, and wasn't the nutrition talk boring?" asked Jack. "We all know pizza is loaded with calories. Yes, it has carbohydrates, but at the expense of 1000 calories. Oh, sorry, Aline, I shouldn't be talking this way your first day here. No secret though as to what we all think about pizza."

Before I got situated, Diane walked over and read my menu. "Where is your mayo?"

"I didn't see it."

"It's on the counter next to the ketchup and mustard packets which are next to the water up there," she pointed the way. "You only need one packet."

I returned to the table with a blue packet of Kraft mayo. I wanted to toss it in the trash, but I couldn't risk such a blatant act the first day.

Grace told me we wouldn't go back to the unit until one o'clock. If we could persuade an intern to go for a turtle-like walk, we'd do that, then just hang out until group therapy at 1:30. She said, "We're divided into two groups for Process, somewhat based on age but also just whatever staff thinks will work best for talking about certain subjects.

"I should mention, too, don't talk about food while we're eating. It's a trigger for some and causes problems. Plus who wants to talk about food when we have to eat it, no matter what? Everyone follows a different meal plan, so just ignore everyone else and focus on your own." Grace seemed to know how to survive the rules of this place. Was she anorexic or bulimic? I couldn't remember.

Everyone pretty much focused on their own plates, but, while some ate quickly, others ate very deliberately. I tried to concentrate on the sandwich. I'd eaten a bagel for breakfast at 6:00 that morning, so I felt hungry now but didn't want to eat a huge sandwich. I opened the 2% milk carton, squeezed the 70 calories of mayo onto the turkey and took a bite. I couldn't imagine finishing in thirty minutes.

The table conversation shifted to favorite movies. I chewed and swallowed. I hadn't drunk milk, except on Frosted Flakes, in months. A sandwich with two slices of bread and cheese was not on my menu at home. Probably 240 calories with all the bread and another 80-100 with the cheese. I wanted to run out of the cafeteria. I didn't know how to channel the panic that gripped me like a noose around my neck.

Diane must have read my mind when she looked at me. "You can take the apple back to the unit. There will be time to finish it before group meets."

What a relief. I quickly swallowed the remainder of the bread, finished the milk, and looked around to see what everyone did with their trays. I stood and started to walk towards the disposal area, but Diane stopped me. "I need to check your tray to make certain you ate everything." She looked under the paper napkin, shook the milk carton. "You're good."

We gathered where this caloric nightmare had begun, at the entrance to the cafeteria. The short walk back to our unit left us standing outside the locked door. We waited for a buzz and click before we entered.

CHAPTER

3

SILENT SCREAM

The Country Club crowd
stands alongside the buffet
nod their approval
of two fish ice sculptures,
platters of shrimp, smoked salmon,
silver containers filled with
scallops, clams, lobster, and mussels.
Servers in white uniform jackets
offer guests their choice of entrees
or *some of everything.*
I want to scream out loud at the display,
I don't do buffets
not because I dislike fish
but because I can't count the calories
to assess how much I should take.
So, I scream silently
select spinach and Caesar salads
a hard roll, no butter,

it's easier and safer to restrict,
let people think I'll go back for more.

CHAPTER 4

As promised, Kathryn found me once we walked back on the unit, behind locked doors. She motioned for me to follow her into her office. "We need to discuss meal plans and menus for the week."

All I could think about was how caged in I felt. Doors remained locked all the time, even bathroom doors. Now food, again, became the focus.

I sat down on the chair next to Kathryn's desk. She shared an office with a therapist and another nutritionist. It was crowded, but Kathryn located a scrap of paper with a number written on it. She glanced at it and pulled out some papers from a desk drawer which looked like menus.

"Based on the weight we got this morning," she held up the scrap of paper, "and the medical information in your chart, you'll need to eventually consume 3500 calories a day in order to get you to a healthy weight. We won't start with 3500 calories, but that is the goal for a safe and steady weight gain within a reasonable amount of time."

My hands began to sweat. My face felt hot. "Three-thousand five-hundreed calories?! I can't possibly eat enough food in a day to equal 3500 calories. Heck, I probably eat less than 1000 calories."

"I realize that, so we begin gradually. Your stomach couldn't handle 3500 calories right now, so we'll look at a meal plan with about 2000 calories for several days. What do you eat for breakfast?" asked Kathryn.

"Either a big bowl of Frosted Flakes or Cheerios with milk or a bagel with peanut butter."

"Since you need a lot of protein right now, go with the bagel and peanut butter and a cup of 2% milk. What do you eat for lunch?"

"A carton of yogurt or maybe a piece of fruit, some peanuts. I don't really need lunch. I'm not hungry, and I don't like to take the time. I have meetings, my workout, housework, cooking and baking."

"You do need to get carbohydrates, proteins, and fats throughout the day, so we'll spread them out and not load them into a single meal. For lunch here in the hospital, let's put you down for a turkey sandwich again tomorrow, then grilled cheese on Thursday and a fish sandwich on Friday. Like today, two slices of bread for carbs, a packet of mayo for fat, the turkey and cheese, and a carton of 2% milk for protein and calcium. For dinner tomorrow night, they're serving Swedish meatballs, which are pretty good here, and noodles. How about some juice? It may be easier to drink calories right now rather than eat a piece of fruit. Do you want cranberry or apple juice? And, the 2% milk of course." She checked things off on the menu forms on her desk. "That just leaves dinner Thursday because Friday's program ends after snack at 2:30 P.M. You eat dinner at home on Fridays. You look skeptical. What are you thinking, Aline?"

I wanted to cry and run out of the room and go home. If I returned to the hospital in the morning—a big *if*—the meals were now planned for days. Except for one dinner. But, I responded with a steady voice. "It seems like a lot of food. What's offered for Thursday's dinner?"

"Lasagna or pork chop. If you select pork chop, you'll still need juice and milk and a roll with butter or potatoes for carbohydrates and fat. With the lasagna you get all the carbs and fats you need in one serving."

"Do I have to eat it all...if I get full?"

"Yes. 100%. You will feel full, but you have to eat the meals. And keep in mind the meals constitute only part of your overall meal plan. You need two snacks on the unit and a snack in the evening after you get home. The only food item you have for snack is an Ensure Plus at 10:30 when you arrive in the mornings and again at snack time in the afternoon. We have plenty of Ensure Plus in the refrigerator," said Kathryn.

"Is it ok if I bring my own Ensure from home? I like a variety of flavors, especially if I now have to drink three a day."

"That's up to you, but they're here if you forget to bring in yours."

If I brought in my Ensures which only contained 220 calories, and which I sometimes drank instead of eating lunch, I could cut out 130 calories every snack because Ensure Plus contained 350 calories. I'd have to be a bit sneaky to get regular Ensure in the refrigerator, but if I brought several in a brown paper bag, it just might work. It was worth the risk to regain some control over what I was forced to eat.

"Keep in mind, Aline, that you shouldn't compare your plate of food or snacks with anyone else. Everyone must finish their meals, and everyone has a different meal plan. You're feeding a starving body. It's going to seem like a lot at first, but you've been eating so little that any increase will feel enormous. It will affect you physically as your stomach adjusts. It takes time. We'll aim for a weight gain of one to two pounds a week," said Kathryn. She collected all the menus and glanced at her watch. "It's time for group Process. You'll be in the room down at the end of the hall, with Grace, Jack, and Madison. I believe Carolyn and Sara are in that group, too. We've split the patients in two mostly based on age."

Kathryn added, "If you need to use the bathroom before group, I'll unlock the one off the art room, which is also the kitchen. Or there's a bathroom down in your group room which Laura or a student intern can unlock. Since you're not bulimic, you don't have to wait two hours after meals before using the bathroom."

Why was that rule necessary?

When I stood up and began to walk down the hall, I realized I still held the apple from lunch. I certainly didn't intend to eat it when we were already scheduled to eat snacks in an hour. I spotted a trash can in the kitchen and tossed the apple beneath some paper napkins.

I walked to the end of the hall. The group room was next to the door I'd entered three hours earlier. The room looked a little bit like a living room, minus table lamps and decorations. Large, padded chairs filled the room. Two windows had curtains, and the lighting was anemic. An enormous solid wood table occupied the center space in the room. Some of the girls who'd gathered used it as a footrest. A couple of large water cups and straws, a box of tissues, some knitting needles, colored pencils and Mandala coloring books rested on the tabletop. Jack sat reading a book. Grace and Madison talked while Madison grabbed the pencils and started to draw. And, sure enough, there was a bathroom. It took a key to enter. I sat down in a chair near the exit door.

Grace looked at me. "Laura is our therapist today, but she's on the phone."

Within a couple of minutes, a business casual-dressed woman with black, curly hair walked through the door and looked around the room. We made eye contact. "Hi," she said. "I'm Laura, one of the therapists here, and today I'm with you all. How has your day been going?"

At the sound of Laura's voice, I noticed Jack looked up from his book, put a finger in to mark his place and said, "I can answer that. The day is the same as every other day." Dressed in black jeans and a black T shirt with a scarf wrapped around his neck and soft facial features, he looked about seventeen or eighteen. His black hair kept falling over his left eye. He looked like a stick figure I might draw.

"Aline, is there one word which describes how you feel now?" asked Laura.

"Probably *relief,* yeah, relief that lunch is over," I said.

"Grace, what about you?"

"*Angry.*" Her eyes returned to her lap.

"Madison?" I couldn't remember, was Madison anorexic? She wasn't skinny like Jack.

"I'm just fine."

"You know *fine* is not a feeling," said Laura. "Say more."

"Okay, *disgusted.*"

Laura turned to Sara, "What word describes your feelings this afternoon?"

"I'm just sleepy. Didn't sleep very well on the hard bed last night. The beds here are so uncomfortable."

Madison interjected, "I'm sick of eating all the time, and lunch is so darn rushed. Today we only had about twenty minutes to eat by the time we got our trays. I have so much to eat; I need more time. Some of the girls don't eat as much food. It's really frustrating."

"Say more about meals in general. What would help you out?" asked Laura.

Madison straightened up in her chair, "First, my meals are too big. Second, you need to get everyone to slow down. A couple of the girls from the other group eat so quickly they've cleared away their trays before I barely get started. They come back and sit down at the table looking bored and staring at me like I'm the one keeping everybody in the cafeteria."

"Do you think you may be too deliberate in eating, which makes you slower? Maybe if you are positioned at the front of the line to get your food, you could get a head start. I'll also tell staff that we need to leave the unit by 12:30, so we get our full thirty minutes for lunch. Is dinner a problem, too?" asked Laura.

"It's not as bad because we seem to get down to the cafeteria by 5:30 pretty easily," said Jack.

I listened and considered whether I ate slowly. I cut my food into small pieces, took small bites. At home I didn't give my pace of eating any thought. I fed our son dinner after swim practice, and John ate whenever he got home from work. I ate last.

"Anyone else want to talk about meals? Not your individual meal plans. Take that up with Kathryn. But are there other issues?" asked Laura.

"Snacks are my big issue," said Carolyn.

I couldn't remember, was Carolyn anorexic?

Dressed in an oversized sweatshirt which hid her actual size she elaborated. "I hate having a snack so close to mealtimes. Who's even hungry at 10:30 and 2:30? There are only ninety minutes between the end of lunch and the afternoon snack. It's not enough time to digest your food and feel hungry. If anything, I feel bloated and have a stomachache after lunch most days. Don't the rest of you feel the same way?"

A chorus of *yes* floated around the room. I thought snacks were unnecessary anytime, but new to the schedule, I didn't realize a snack followed so soon after lunch.

"The eating disorder unit is assigned specific times to eat in the cafeteria in the same way the other behavioral units have specific mealtimes. Snacks are spaced out so there's approximately two hours between a meal and the snack. Remember gang, you're all here because of an eating disorder and recovery depends upon refeeding, getting your bodies to a healthy spot and eating regularly and consistently. You don't want to put the calories from snacks onto your lunch and dinner plates, so we spread your intake of food throughout the day," said Laura.

Jack set his book on the floor. "Can we talk about something else? You forgot to ask me how I'm feeling now and, frankly, I feel crappy. I probably have the most food to eat in a day, even more than you, Madison. But, you just have to do it if you want to get out of here...before insurance runs out or you get so far behind in school, it's impossible to get caught up."

"Take last night. My snack got screwed up by the kitchen, but what am I going to do about it at eight o'clock? I told Sheila, the night nurse, but she couldn't get a different snack. The kitchen's closed. And, all the guys from the behavioral unit came into our unit to watch television. It got loud so I went to my room to read. Then I did something which broke my string of four days, I purged. No one knew, until now. See, Laura, I'm being honest about it."

"Wasn't your bathroom door locked?" asked Laura.

"I'd asked Sheila to unlock it, so I could shower. She didn't know anything about it." He paused. "I'll start a new streak today."

I hoped my mouth was closed as I listened to Jack explain what he'd done. Why would he admit to purging? I didn't know anyone who purged regularly. I thought about how glad I was to sleep in my own bed at home and use the bathroom whenever I wanted and not worry about getting the wrong snack or being locked out of the bathroom. This place scared me, and all I could think about was how quickly I could get discharged from the outpatient program.

I stared at Jack who didn't smile. His eyes were dark, and he'd spoken softly. His gestures were somewhat effeminate, the way he crossed his legs and used his hands and arms to talk. I wanted to get to know him better. He looked around the same age as my youngest son.

Laura's questions brought me back to the moment. "What do you think triggered you to purge: the snack mix-up, the patients from the other unit, a phone call with your dad? Did you have an opportunity to talk with your brother, Tommy?"

"It was probably a combination of things. And, the opportunity to purge presented itself, and I took advantage of it," said Jack.

"You realize, I'll have to let Sheila know and tell the rest of the staff. To keep you safe, we'll need to make some adjustments," said Laura.

Carolyn said, "I hear the other group down the hall getting snacks, so they're finished with Process. Can we go now, too?"

Laura looked at her watch. "It is 2:25. Does anyone else have something urgent to talk about? If so, we can finish in my office. If not, you can go get your snacks. We have art today at three o'clock."

I stood up and followed the group into the hall to the art room/kitchen to get an Ensure Plus. I hoped it would be my last *Plus.*

CHAPTER

5

STARVED SPIRIT

He strolls into the hospital cafeteria
in black tennis shoes, dark T-shirt
and jeans too big for his hips;
clipped of his long black hair
the short cut discloses
hollow cheeks, sunken eyes.
Since his last discharge five months ago
his ribs and shoulder blades
press against that thin shirt.
Will consuming more this time around
yield a lasting recovery?

CHAPTER 6

In the kitchen, all the girls crowded around the refrigerator. I stood back and waited. I wasn't in a hurry. "I need one protein, two carbs," said someone. Another said she needed two carbs, a fruit, calcium and on and on it went. Girls walked away with individual cottage cheese containers, string cheese, yogurt, apples, packs of Lorna Doons, chips, individual boxes of cereal and Gatorade. No one held an Ensure Plus in their hand, and I didn't see any in the refrigerator. I hoped they'd run out. The intern in the room looked up from the snack list. She compared it with what everyone held in their hands. "Aline, the Ensure Plus are kept in the room where staff meets. Come with me and I'll get you one. Do you want chocolate or vanilla? Do you want it over ice?"

"Chocolate. Am I the only one drinking Ensure?"

"Currently, yes, but it changes all the time. Just depends who needs a complete supplement. Do you want a straw?"

With my drink in hand, we walked back to the room where my day had begun. Everyone spread out. I found a chair next to Jack. He balanced a bowl full of cottage cheese on his lap and squeezed a packet of cream cheese over it with his right hand, added two packets of black pepper, then emptied a small box of Fruit Loops on top of that. He stirred it all together.

I stared. It looked disgusting. I needed to know, "Do you eat this much for all your snacks every day?"

"Yeah, I don't want to add more food to my meals, so my snacks are pretty big. At least I don't have an Ensure today."

"They're not so bad, cold. And it goes down quickly."

"I'll give you that. But I don't care for them," he said as he spooned a mouthful of the concoction into his mouth. The cottage cheese turned colors, thanks to the Fruit Loops.

"You're inpatient, right?" I asked. "What's it like?" I drank the Ensure through the straw. I was actually thirsty, so it tasted pretty good, although I wouldn't admit that to anyone. I frequently substituted an Ensure for lunch at home to avoid the stress of thinking about and fixing something more complicated than opening a bottle.

"Well, the restrictions get to you after a while: no phone or computer, locked bathroom doors. Weekends are the toughest part. There's not any programming, so it's really boring."

"Can you at least watch television or movies? Go outside for walks?"

"We usually watch a movie or two on Saturday night."

"Are you in school?" I asked as I drank more and he kept eating Fruit Loops and cottage cheese.

"Yeah, I'm a senior. But I may not graduate in June, thanks to my frequent stays here. I dropped a class and may drop another which means I'll make them up in summer school."

"How do you manage to keep up with homework?"

"My folks bring me stuff. Tommy, my brother gets assignments from the teachers. He's in ninth grade, so we're at the same high school."

I finished the Ensure and stood to throw away the empty cup, but before I did, Jack pointed out that I needed to show the intern I'd finished it.

A tall woman walked into the room. She had shoulder length, thick, black hair and wore large-framed glasses on a chain around her neck. Several of the girls greeted Suzanne. She walked up to me and introduced herself as the head of the eating disorder unit. She explained she'd attended meetings all day so didn't have a chance to meet with me until snack time. She motioned for me to follow her.

Her office was in a corner down another hall "Have a seat." I sat down across from her at her desk. I noticed two things about the room. Papers and books on the topic of eating disorders, mental health, cognitive behavior and new techniques for treating anorexia covered every corner of the desk. And, there were countless wall hangings which conveyed sentiments about recovery, persistence, body image, beauty and health. The entire office was like a museum from prior patients' recovery efforts.

"So, Aline, tell me, why did you decide to come in today? Why now?" Suzanne sat back in her chair.

I repeated the story I'd told in group during the morning introductions.

"Well, I know your weight, and I'm glad you decided to come in. You should be inpatient, but I understand that you wouldn't go along with that ,so we'll work with you as an outpatient. And it *will* be work."

It was *work just* to get here. I wasn't certain what she meant.

"Kathryn knows what she's talking about when it comes to nutrition and what it takes to refeed a starved body, so follow her meal plans. The weight gain will be slow as your metabolism kicks into gear. You may even lose a pound before you get going because your body will be working hard to use what you're giving it."

I smiled to myself. I wouldn't mind losing a pound or two.

I began to realize that coming into the hospital daily wouldn't be a short-term commitment. My mind raced ahead to my schedule for the next couple of weeks, especially between the hours of 10:30 A.M. and 6:00 P.M. When would I get anything accomplished? How would I explain my absences at book club, Bible study, school meetings? Most importantly, how would I get dinners prepared for the family Monday through Thursday?

Suzanne interrupted my anxious thoughts. "Aline, have you met Grace, she's been here, off and on, inpatient and outpatient, and she will be able to answer most of your questions about the program and the routine. Grace's story is complicated, but she's more mature than some of the teenagers, so are Madison and Carolyn. That's why I put you in the group you found yourself in today. Some topics which come up aren't really appropriate for the teenagers." Suzanne leaned forward and said in a softer voice, "I do want to caution you about one thing. Don't get involved in everyone's situation to the point you lose focus of your own recovery. I know you have a family, and you'll want to *mother* these girls and Jack. Try not to. It won't help you."

How was I going to turn off my role as a *mother?* That's what I was and most of these patients just might need some TLC.

We concluded our talk, and I walked to the art room. Everyone was cutting words, which depicted emotions, from magazines. What was the point of this activity? A time filler or some sort of therapy for the teenagers? I didn't need to cut out words to express how I felt, but I grabbed a scissors and a magazine to look for the words *scared, sad, angry*. I kept reminding myself to play along with the game here in the hospital. At 4:30 P.M. we cleaned up the scraps of paper and headed back to the larger group room.

"Everyone, grab a check-out sheet and give them back to me," said Elyse.

I asked Grace, "So what are we doing?"

She explained we filled out the form each day to indicate what we'd do after dinner, what our snack plans were, what might serve as a distraction. No big deal. Just put down what I'd be doing at home. At five o'clock, we got ready for dinner and were met by Suzanne and Laura in the hall.

Dinner mirrored lunch. I grabbed utensils, 2% milk, and the tray with my menu on it. Ella still served the food. She glanced at my menu and smiled, handed me a plate completely covered with meatballs, noodles, and gravy. I felt my knees start to buckle. I'd not eaten such a quantitiy of food at one time in years. I walked to our group table, sat down, and stared at the noodles.

I sat next to a petite woman with short hair and glasses, which she only used to read. She appeared closer to my age of 58, probably in her forties. She wore faded blue jeans and an oversized, blue hoodie. "Hi," I managed to say. "You're Carolyn, right?"

She nodded as she buttered a roll.

What could I do about all these noodles? Hide them, but where?

"Sorry I didn't talk with you today," she said. "I've got lots of insurance problems, and we've been working through them all day. Coverage won't last much longer, maybe just through Friday unless Diane can convince the insurance company I need to stay." She opened her milk carton and drank from it without using a straw. If I tried that I'd spill down the front of my shirt. She cut into what looked like meatloaf and a baked potato with butter, took a small bite and frowned.

"Insurance can force you out? I guess I didn't think about that aspect of treatment," I said, as I looked at my two large meatballs. I considered my limited options. If I wanted to get out of the program as soon as possible and still retain my physician, I'd comply for now. I cut a meatball into quarters and forked meat into my mouth.

"Do you live near the hospital?" I asked in an effort to make conversation after I swallowed and took a drink of milk.

"Not really, I live on the east side, close to where I work. Just me and my dog, Charlie."

"What do you do about the dog when you're here all day long?"

"A neighbor who likes Charlie takes him outside twice a day and gives him food and water. Do you have a dog?" She cut into the meat loaf and took another bite.

"No, but I'm married and have four sons. One is still in high school." I stabbed some noodles and discovered the flavor with the gravy tasted almost as good as the Swedish meatballs I made at Christmas.

Suzanne sat down across from Carolyn and stated she was certain the insurance issue was resolved through next Tuesday. A lone salad bowl sat on Suzanne's tray. She noticed my questioning look. "I have a dinner meeting tonight, Aline, so this is a snack." I wondered if maybe I should offer her some of my noodles.

Suzanne turned to Jack, "I understand we need a new procedure concerning locked bathrooms. How did today go?"

"Okay. My folks are coming after dinner tonight, bringing more homework and another book or two."

I kept eating noodles, but the quantity didn't seem to diminish on the plate. I looked at the clock. 5:45 already. At least others still sat eating. Just after 6:00, we disposed of the trays but not before a quick check for hidden noodles or uneaten food. My stomach felt so full I thought I might get sick.

Back on the unit, on the other side of the locked door, the inpatients dispersed to their rooms, while the outpatients gathered their gear and headed for the back door to exit. Diane stood ready to unlock it. "See you all tomorrow morning. Remember to have your snack when you get home tonight."

I'd already forgotten about that. Meatballs and noodles occupied my mind and stomach. Maybe I'd forget about the snack altogether. Who would know, besides me? Why was it so difficult to be honest about food? I pulled the car keys from my pocket and slipped into the safe space of my car where no one could tell me what to eat.

CHAPTER

7

COMMON THREADS

Control. Restrict. Eating disorders. Anorexia and bulimia. Shoulder blades press against clothes. Low self-esteem causes isolation, abandoned dreams, friends' ostracism. Meal plans and snacks based upon individualized caloric needs are calculated upon hospitalization. Patients' pulse rates increase with daily weight checks, fear of even the slightest weight gain is a thread tying everyone together. Panic grips patients with mandatory snacks, including Jack who copes by spreading soft cream cheese on cottage cheese, sprinkling on two packets of black pepper, mixing with Fruit Loops, Cheerios or crumbled bran muffins. At lunch food is not discussed, simply eaten, with eyes on one's own plate but the 2% milk, buttered rolls, puddings, pies, meatballs, and pasta elicit tension even before glancing at someone who cuts a turkey sandwich with a knife and fork into miniscule bites or another who pours taco sauce on a grilled cheese.

Patient compliance doesn't end with presentation of an empty plate to student interns, they explore the entire tray looking for food in wadded up paper napkins, in milk cartons, under plates and bowls, beneath the foil lid of a Smuckers' peanut butter packet because, if 100% of the meal isn't completed, an Ensure is chugged. Besides deception's deployment surrounding food, hoodies and bulky clothes hide emaciated bodies and cuttings while therapy strives to ascertain the issues, feelings behind rapes, molestations, abortions, abuse, parental expectations, obsessive exercise, overuse of diuretics. In sharing experiences from the outside and commiserating about the restrictions while on the unit, light shines on deeply guarded secrets. Afraid of weight gain, the similarly situated break walls of silence, build trust. Treatment tolerated with hope of recovery not death. Relapse likely but tools identified. Focus on facts. Control fears. Replenish. Restore.

CHAPTER

8

At 9:30 A.M. the following morning, I left the house to drive to the hospital. I thought about all the rules, restrictions, and my plan to get regular Ensures into the staff refrigerator. The anxiety I felt was different from the previous day. Now I knew what to expect and really didn't want to go, but I knew deep down I needed help with my weight loss. Heavy traffic and limited parking spaces meant it was 10:25 before I buzzed the door to the hospital. Diane let me inside. "Glad you came back, Aline. Cold enough for you?"

"It's too cold when the temperature goes below freezing. I brought some Ensure from home, different flavors. Should I put them in the staff refrigerator?"

"I'll put them on a shelf for you. I see you put your name on the paper bag, so there won't be any confusion. Do you want to grab one now, since it's snack time?"

I hadn't even taken off my jacket, and I was being told to eat. "Yes," I said, "I'll take a strawberry over ice, please."

We headed down to the staff room. After getting my Ensure, I walked into the larger group room where everyone opened their snacks. Diane didn't say a word about the calorie count on my Ensure bottle. What a relief. I felt confident I could keep up the deceit about the Ensure switch if I used a paper bag and offered to get it myself. I smiled inside.

Several patients selected individual cereal boxes. Cheerios were popular, probably because they contained fewer calories than a sugar-coated cereal. I picked up a sheet of paper off the chair next to Madison. "Morning. What am I supposed to do with this?"

"Write what you actually did last night, whether you ate a snack, whether you ate breakfast, that sort of thing," she said.

A blond woman full of energy and enthusiasm strode into the room. She stood next to the chair in which everyone piled the papers with scribbled notes. "Good morning, gang. Missed you yesterday, but I needed a day of vacation. You guys wear me out. Who wants to start with check-in?"

"I'll start, Jenny," said Carly. She talked about watching television on the unit and eating her snack. She said she'd probably gotten eight hours of sleep, showered, and went to breakfast this morning. Everyone else described their evening and morning routines. I didn't hear anything jaw-dropping, but I learned not everyone ate their snacks and some didn't finish breakfast.

While I listened, it occurred to me that, since I wasn't accountable to anyone at home, I could lie at these morning check-ins. No one here would know what took place at my house. But I'd followed the rules the night before. So, I had no reason to lie today. "When I got home, I fixed supper for my husband, checked on my son to make certain he'd eaten and completed his homework, did a load of laundry, ate my snack when John ate dessert. Slept about six or seven hours, ate breakfast, and here I am."

"Good job for the first night at home, Aline," said Jenny.

I watched everyone eat snacks while I drank my Ensure. Tracy spread peanut butter on toast, and, of course, Jack stirred cottage cheese, cream cheese and, today, a muffin in a bowl. An Ensure Plus sat on the floor next to his feet. I wondered why the Ensure showed up on his meal plan. Would my snack begin to include solid foods? Student interns walked around and double-checked containers and food wrappers to make certain snacks were consumed.

At 11:30, Jenny announced we'd spend the education hour discussing causes of eating disorders until lunch. She passed around printed copies of some study, and we talked about psychological, interpersonal, social, and biological factors which contributed to eating disorders. Jenny highlighted low self-esteem. Nearly every hand went up when she asked the group if they felt like they experienced low self-esteem. I'd heard a lot of the same information before, but it came across differently in the hospital environment.

Lack of control in one's life, depression, anxiety—even anger—were shown to be factors. Data indicated some tendencies were inherited. I related to everything everyone said. A common denominator surfaced within the group. Maybe we were more alike than I realized. The hour passed quickly before lunch time.

Jenny and two interns walked us to the cafeteria. Nothing changed from the previous day. The crowded, noisy room smelled of fried foods. I fell into line, grabbed silverware, napkin, and a 2% milk carton. Jenny handed my tray to me with the meal plan on it. Cranberry juice stared at me. Well, I thought, at least I could drink it more quickly than I could eat an apple. A plated grilled cheese sandwich appeared. I decided it wouldn't be so bad when I looked around and saw that everyone else had a lot more food on their trays: salads with regular dressings, pieces of fruit, tomato soup, puddings, cake.

We sat at long tables pushed together with the staff scattered among us checking, always checking, our plates. Madison sat next to me with two Smuckers' peanut butter packets but no bread. What was she planning to do with the peanut butter? I tried to remain focused on my grilled cheese and juice. I couldn't remember when I'd last eaten a grilled cheese sandwich. When I finally took a bite, to my surprise, it tasted great. The eating disorder inside my head told me sandwiches were full of fat, so I'd stopped eating them at home. Several people at the table ate grilled cheese with a cup of tomato soup. I wished I could eat soup but couldn't because the eating disorder said *NO.* I didn't need the calories in the creamy tomato soup. I'd already eaten enough with the grilled cheese.

Meanwhile, Madison looked at a pasta-based casserole on her plate. She cut an apple into slices and spread peanut butter on each slice. She spread the remaining peanut butter onto her brownie. I hoped my meals wouldn't require such creativity in order to meet protein requirements.

Jenny reminded everyone we'd have Process at 1:30. I really didn't understand the point of talking for an hour in Process. Was everyone honest about their situation? How much should I share with girls young enough to be my daughters? It felt awkward.

At 1:30, I joined my group in the room at the end of the hall. Two girls were curled up under blankets while Madison pulled out her fine tip pencils and a sketch book. She brought life to the page on which she worked. "You certainly have an eye for color and shape, Madison," I said.

"I love to paint but drawing is good, too. It's a hobby of mine. I'll show you what I'm working on in the art room if you're interested. I'll paint when the rest of you go to yoga at three o'clock," she said.

Before I could ask about yoga, Suzanne walked into the room, pushed her black-framed glasses onto the top of her head and sat down directly across from Madison and me. "How was lunch? Anybody have anything they want to talk about?" She paused. "Maybe something will surface if we go around the room and check in with one word, other than *fine.*"

We each responded quickly until we got to Madison. She looked down at the floor. "What's going on, Madison?" asked Suzanne.

"I'm having flashbacks. They occurred again last night. It was hard to go back to sleep, so I'm sleep deprived today." She began to cry. "Actually, the dreams are terrible, and then I get angry thinking about how even after all these years, he holds power over me, even if it's just in dreams. It's horrible enough that he took something from me, but it goes on and on."

I grabbed the box of tissues from the table and handed it to Madison.

"How far back do the dreams take you?" asked Suzanne.

What was Madison talking about? I was clueless. *He* who? What did the individual take? Her virginity possibly, but she was only in her early twenties now, and she said this occurred years ago.

Madison continued, "The dreams go back to the school bus. Then there are police sirens out on the street, a gunshot...it's so vivid."

Suzanne said the two of them would talk further after Process, and so that was that. I wanted to know what she was talking about, but I couldn't very well just come out and ask. Maybe one of the other patients who knew Madison better than I did could fill me in.

Suzanne directed her attention to Grace and asked, "Can you find a substitute teacher for school next week? It looks like insurance will cover another week of treatment for you."

"Yes, I can. I know I'm not ready to go back into my high school classroom. Thanks for getting insurance to give the okay," said Grace.

Sara asked whether the group could go for more walks, even if it was cold. Sara was cute with short brown hair. She was probably in her late twenties and very athletic. "When I get home after being here all day, I go for a brisk walk, and then I walk in the morning but that's not enough exercise."

"Sara, I know you're permitted to walk in moderation, 10-15 minutes at a time. But if you're going on hour long walks, power walks, or jogging, you need to increase your food intake. Until you can keep your weight up and not drop pounds, you need to cut back on the exercise. It's not forever," said Suzanne.

Suzanne looked at the clock and then at me. 2:20. "Have you shared with the group why you're here?"

"A little. I've lost weight and..."

"Granted, but why have you come in now?"

"The cause for the weight loss goes back several decades," I began. "My sister became ill suddenly, was admitted into the hospital on a Friday night and died early Tuesday morning. She developed pneumonia and spiked a fever of 108 degrees. Her brain died before her body gave up. She left behind a husband and two young children." I realized I hadn't taken a breath. I paused and looked around the room.

Everyone stared at me.

"My parents' first child had died at age two. With the death of my thirty-year-old sister, their second child, I became the lone survivor at age twenty-four. My parents suffocated me with love and also fear. I couldn't sneeze without them asking whether I was sick."

"Aline, I'm sorry but we have to stop here. It's already past time to get started on snacks." Suzanne stood up and headed towards her office. Madison gathered her art supplies and followed her.

I relaxed my shoulders. I didn't realize I'd been so tense while I recounted the death of my sister. I didn't even know why I'd revealed so much. It probably didn't matter except it made me feel vulnerable. Everyone seemed to hold secrets tightly. Perhaps I wouldn't be called upon to share anymore, which was a relief, but, also somewhat frustrating because I'd shared a lot then was told to stop.

Everyone drifted out of the room and went to get snacks. No drama with snacks, today.

I learned that only about half of the group participated in the yoga. I'd never given it a try, so figured I would. At least this activity got me up and moving instead of sitting for another hour. Additionally, we got to leave the unit to go to a different room. I didn't understand why everyone wasn't required to participate. Maybe it was too much exercise for some.

The instructor, Lucy, was calm, soft spoken, caring, and cautious about our group's level of activity. At four o'clock, we rolled up our mats and returned to the unit. Jack was reading, some painted and others just talked.

Shortly, everyone grabbed check-out forms and began to list goals for the evening, how they would be achieved, what could get in the way, and what could be done to make certain we'd actually eat evening snacks. I was tired and wanted to get through dinner and drive home. I did not want to prepare dinner for John. I was sick of looking at and talking about food and eating things I didn't want to eat. Laundry and house cleaning awaited. Apparently, so did an Ensure.

I really didn't care what appeared on my plate for Thursday's dinner in the cafeteria. We headed out the unlocked door and walked down the hall past the bright vending machines.

CHAPTER 9

PERFECT DAUGHTER

The older neighbor boy molested her
in the back of the school bus
day after day
he threatened harm to her sister if she told.
She aborted a fetus
kept that secret.
She ran
from the image in her bathroom mirror;
eye make-up and hoodie couldn't hide the loss
of self-esteem and weight below ninety pounds;
her mother was proud of her slender body,
her straight A's and virginity until marriage.
But another victim talked,
police sirens alerted the rapist
who hid in his barn with a shotgun.
She heard the single gunshot.

CHAPTER 10

I drove to the hospital Friday morning knowing I wouldn't eat dinner there. John, our son, and I could eat together at home or go out. They'd probably want pizza, and I could eat a slice, but I'd think about other options for myself throughout the day. Friday was a day for choices. I intended to make some.

Check-in wasn't particularly noteworthy. I got an Ensure and a check-in form, found a seat and tried to remain inconspicuous. Education focused on the differences in the way males and females presented an eating disorder case. Laura led the discussion and explained that while it's considered a woman's disease, it's not. Guys are under-reported. There's a social stigma so guys don't seek treatment as much, and it's not as easy to detect.

At 12:30 we walked down the hallway, past the vending machines, and headed to the cafeteria and lunch. It wasn't as crowded, but it smelled of fried fish. Ella handed me a plated fish sandwich which meant a bun with its 150 calories. Add mayo, cranberry juice, and 2% milk and the calorie count soared to at least 600 with the fried fish. I didn't eat this amount for dinner, my biggest meal of the day before coming into the hospital.

I felt a bit of joy when I took a bite of the fish sandwich. I hadn't eaten a hot sandwich in months. But, when experiencing this pleasure, I felt guilty. How could I like and enjoy something I didn't need? I didn't want the additional calories. I couldn't rationalize the need for calories when I feared eating too much and losing control.

After lunch we returned to group Process then snack. The outpatients ate their snacks quickly, so they could leave. I caught on and headed for the exit door with the others. "Don't forget to eat those snacks over the weekend. See you Monday morning," said Diane.

Once outside I took a deep breath and told myself I was free.

A swim meet, house cleaning, laundry, church, and a walk filled the weekend, but, by late Sunday afternoon I felt anxious about returning to the hospital the next morning. I'd followed my meal plan and eaten snacks, but not all of the snacks required. Drinking Ensure in the afternoon and evening wasn't too difficult, but the morning Ensure was a stretch. I attended church during Sunday's scheduled Ensure and didn't make it up. My portion sizes at meals were not the equivalent of those at the hospital. I felt panic. My stomach turned. What if I'd lost a pound? John grilled chicken for dinner Sunday night, but anxiety prevented me from eating much.

How could I complete the check-in form Monday morning? I debated whether I needed to explain everything. I decided to state that I'd eaten all my meals and snacks. I just wouldn't state that I didn't have every snack. It wasn't a lie; it was an omission of a fact. No one would ask, I felt certain. No one had challenged my regular Ensure substitution for Ensure Plus. I felt guilty, but the fear of gaining weight was stronger than the fear of telling a small lie. I needed to formulate a plan.

I couldn't find a parking space Monday morning at the hospital. Maybe I could use that as an excuse to turn around and drive home. On-street parking was the only option, and even that meant a three-block walk. By the time I entered the hospital, everyone else gathered in the large room across from the nurses' station, selected snacks, and picked up check-in sheets. I just sat down with my Ensure when nurse Sharon asked me to follow her. Oh, of course, the Monday weight check. I complied then returned to the room. At home, my scale indicated I'd dropped a half pound since the week before. I felt a secret pride that I could lose considering the quantity of food I'd eaten at the hospital.

As Jack and the girls took turns describing the weekend, they mentioned some struggles with the meal plans and snacks. There'd been over-exercising, purging, intoxication or something close to it, and an indifferent attitude about the notion of recovery. Jack's parents visited and that seemed to trigger something depressing for him. He ate his snack slowly which was out of character, and he was quiet and withdrawn. Tracy went to a party Saturday night and failed to meet her meet the meal plan or snack requirements. Sara not only went for two walks each day but did some running. She admitted she didn't add anything to her meal plan which she was told to do if she exercised. I felt almost proud of my weekend after listening to others, even though I knew I'd slipped, too. It was almost noon before we finished check-in, so the education discussion consisted of a brief overview of a handout about the potential consequences of living with anorexia and instructions to read it before Wednesday.

Before I could line up for the short walk to the cafeteria, Kathryn came up to me and said, "Aline, your weight dropped over the weekend."

Yes, I thought, proud of myself. I still retained some control.

"That could be because of a couple of things: your activity level increased at home more than you realized, and your portion sizes at meals weren't adequate. Or, your metabolism finally caught fire and you're burning more calories. I'll add some calories into your diet, more carbohydrates and fats. You'll need to eat a bag of potato chips or pretzels at lunch, starting today. I'll add a roll and butter or potatoes at dinners and a carbohydrate at snacks. That's in addition to your Ensure."

I panicked. My stomach felt queasy. I wanted to get my jacket and leave. Emotionally, I was caught off guard with the sudden addition of unnecessary and unwanted calories. But I couldn't do anything about it. Cereal, chips, or cookies with Ensure, really?! Multiply that times three. More carbs and fats at lunch and dinner. I really wanted to tell my therapist she couldn't make me stay here. The buzz and click of the unit door brought me back to reality. I couldn't physically leave the building, but perhaps I'd check-out mentally. Potato chips, probably not even kettle cooked, awaited in the cafeteria. The calories mounted.

An unmistakable yellow bag of Lay's chips sat on my tray, alongside the turkey and cheese sandwich, cranberry juice, and 2% milk. I grabbed a packet of mayo and sat down. Kathryn sat at the end of the table. I opened the bag and took out a few chips and ate them. The salt tasted good. But it was lunch, and I didn't eat chips for lunch. I saved them for dinner. I restricted at lunch and saved up my allotment of calories for dinner. That's just what I did. I felt guilty eating chips at lunch because they added something positive and enjoyable to the meal. What if I couldn't stop? I didn't want to feel pleasure and satisfaction when eating.

Back on our unit we held group Process, and the patients chatted in the hall about whether the staff would hold serious discussions about our not slipping on the weekends, whether inpatient or outpatient. Suzanne was the staff leader for our group, and she zeroed in on each one of us. She wanted to know how I'd lost weight.

I twisted in my chair. "I probably didn't eat large enough portions at mealtimes, but I didn't miss any meals. I did more jobs around the house; I certainly was more active than here at the hospital. Got snacks in," I said.

"Well, Kathryn put together a plan to increase your caloric intake, gradually. But, you're going to have to work on your weekend meals. You don't want to take two steps forward during the week and then take one step back on the weekend. It will take months to put on adequate weight if that happens," said Suzanne as she turned her attention to Madison.

I hadn't lied exactly. I simply didn't disclose that I'd missed a snack and didn't eat a sufficient number of calories at meals. The guilt gnawed at me, but I felt better when the attention shifted to others. We stopped at 2:30 P.M. Time for snacks. Something needed to be added to my Ensure. My adrenaline kicked in, My heart pounded. I wanted to find a low-calorie carbohydrate. I knew no one would take one of my Ensures, so I stopped in the kitchen first to look for something that would meet my requirements. The staff replenished the cereal boxes, so I grabbed a box of Cheerios. Sure enough, there were only 90 calories in a box. That number plus my regular Ensure still provided fewer than the 350 calories in an Ensure Plus, which staff thought I was drinking anyway. This mental game of calorie counting and deceit by omission exhausted me.

I told myself I liked Cheerios for breakfast occasionally, with milk, but the other side of my brain said I didn't need them as a snack. Consumption slowed down. The student intern checked the box before I threw it away. The feeling of a full stomach scared me. I loosened my belt buckle a notch. We'd eat dinner in two hours.

After snacks, we headed to the art room for some painting or drawing. I couldn't draw a straight line with a ruler, let alone paint freehand. But the assignment was to paint something that reflected how we felt about our eating disorder at the moment. I attempted to paint a sailboat in stormy water which reflected my view of going through the treatment process in a stressful environment.

After check-out, like followers of the Pied Piper, we walked to the cafeteria for dinner. I wasn't hungry. I recalled that one of the dinner options was something oriental served over rice. I'd selected the fried chicken option but immediately regretted that choice. In order to comply with 100% of the meal plan, I'd need to eat the fried skin. I didn't eat chicken skin. Plus, I had a roll, butter, and a serving of roasted potatoes on my plate. What if I refused to eat? Would I simply drink an Ensure as a substitute? I needed to ask the others what happened if I wouldn't eat the fried chicken skin. The food consumption expectations felt out of control. I again considered walking out, but no one would help me go through the door to leave. The staff wanted us to talk about feelings. But I didn't want to talk. I buttered the roll and started to take a few bites. Several at the table appeared anxious, so a non-food topic came up: television shows on Monday nights.

It was six o'clock before everyone finished, and my thoughts fast-forwarded to the issue of my evening snack. I could put it off until nine o'clock, but then I'd feel full all night. I couldn't imagine eating a snack before then, however. So, I thought about what I would write down on the check-in form the following morning if I didn't have a snack, at all.

Tuesday morning at the hospital I completed the form and ate my Cheerios and drank an Ensure. I continued to bring strawberry and chocolate and even butter pecan flavored Ensures in every Monday morning in a brown paper bag. Nobody noticed the switch I'd made from drinking Ensure Plus to regular Ensure. I surmised that because I was a mother and more mature, I wasn't viewed as a rule-breaker. No one took the time to take notice. Snacks followed education, and a repetition of *eat, talk, eat, activity, eat* went on and on.

Two weeks later more calories found their way into my diet. More carbohydrates and fats meant dessert. I could choose to have it at lunch or dinner but not as a substitute for the Ensure. I could even pick what I wanted. Ice cream seemed like a good choice until I realized I had to eat two cups of ice cream, not one. Other options included double crusted pies, overly frosted cakes, and super-large cookies. Packages of Lorna Doones became my go-to because the calories were stated on the package. I felt some control over my calorie count.

We weren't allowed to have caffeine, so regular coffee was out of the question. I never understood that rule, but decaf didn't help me stay awake in groups. I didn't know if I felt tired all the time because of caffeine withdrawal or something else, but I felt full all the time.

John supported my participation in the eating disorder program. He actually seemed relieved that I'd taken the initiative. But fear kept me from really committing to it. Gaining weight was the big fear. I believed I didn't need to gain weight. I felt like I was in control of my life, running a household and doing what millions of mothers did. Perhaps I was thinner than the mothers with whom I came in contact, but I believed I was disciplined. I didn't need professionals telling me I wasn't healthy.

Society said women needed to lose weight, all the time, in every form of media: television, radio, magazines, advertisements on billboards. I achieved that societal goal. Other women frequently came up to me and commented they wished they had my problem, of not being able to gain weight. They'd ask if I ate. I said I did but what they couldn't understand and what I didn't explain was I couldn't eat what I wanted to eat. It seemed impossible to convince myself that I needed to gain weight when others were envious of my thin figure.

I reached a crossroad. Either I bought into the treatment program, or I stopped and managed my weight on my own. But if I stopped, I didn't know how I'd get prescriptions for antidepressants. If I gave-in and complied with everyone's rules, I'd gain weight, but I could always lose it. I knew how to restrict really well. I figured I could regain control after I attained the weight everyone wanted me to gain.

CHAPTER

11

ASSAULTED

She hauled a battered backpack
into group therapy,
sat down in an overstuffed armchair
and cried into her hands:
Maybe it never happened.
He has dementia now,
confrontation is pointless.
Flashbacks of childhood molestations
Intensified with the passage of time:
I wonder if Mother knew.
She searched for love in a nunnery
but her spirit broke,
when her female partner left with another
depression engulfed her like a tsunami.
Obsessive exercise,
peanut butter sandwiches,
shots of whiskey
numbed her shame, her loneliness.

After group therapy one day she phoned
from the rocky Lake Michigan shore,
the sound of pounding waves
nearly wiped out her voice:
I don't want to fight anymore.
Purged Guilt

CHAPTER

12

WHY ARE YOU HERE?

In group therapy in her broken English
she whispers *date rape;*
afraid of her father's reaction
the abortion remains a secret.
She binges on her mother's Mexican burritos,
Whoppers and French fries
then purges behind closed doors
terrified of gaining weight.
Self-inflicted cuts on her arms and wrists
contrast with the silver charms –
bullet, hand cuffs, padlock –
dangling from a bracelet.
Her purple fingernails loosen the purple scarf
which accentuates her black attire
and long black hair with pink, violet and turquoise streaks.
Mascara and black eye liner draw my attention
to her look of desperation when the bathroom doors lock
for two hours

after group lunch on the unit.
As the clock ticks away one hundred twenty minutes
she folds strips of pink and purple paper
Into miniscule stars - two thousand every day.

CHAPTER 13

During Process sessions, the therapists probed for deep, buried secrets in order to find their source. Everyone seemed to reveal something, at some point, over the course of a week. But, insurance limits forced many out of the treatment program before they were equipped to leave.

I worked hard to determine the initial trigger for my anorexia. Throughout my 20's, even before my sister died, thoughts of food filled my head. When sitting in Process at the hospital in my 50's, I was forced to return to my law school experience: the feelings of insecurity, my lack of confidence, fear of a loss of control. I couldn't be perfect, but I could master what I ate. I proved to myself I *was* in control with a ten-pound weight loss which stabilized.

My thirty-year-old sister developed diabetes during her first pregnancy when only twenty. She and the baby nearly died, but she maintained control of her blood sugar levels through daily injections of insulin and scrupulous monitoring of her food intake. She ran, was active in her family's life and that of the Air Force community in which they lived. She maintained a perfect weight for ten years. But, her immune system was compromised. Her husband came home with a cold on a Thursday, she caught it and passed early Tuesday morning. There was the trigger for my eating disorder, or was it?

There were further discussions over the course of the next several weeks in Process. While the patient population changed constantly, everyone dug into their secret caverns. But, privacy constraints and time constraints resulted in more unanswered questions than answered questions. Similar causes and responses surfaced, and people became more willing to share.

Carolyn talked about being molested by her father when she was young. She didn't know whether or not her mother even knew. As she got older, she explored the possibility of becoming a nun, but that didn't work out well. She found some satisfaction and happiness in working with kids but couldn't get beyond her trauma in childhood. She formed a female relationship that soured. She got a dog for companionship, but she controlled her life through alcohol and food restrictions: she ate little and drank too much. She'd check into the hospital periodically when her weight dropped and she became depressed and suicidal. She seemed to always be at the mercy of the insurance company, too.

Madison's story continued to unfold, and it was something out of a horror movie. A neighbor boy molested her repeatedly on the school bus. He threatened to do the same thing to her younger sister if she reported him. She kept that secret then added another when she endured an abortion. She didn't tell her parents anything. She was the *perfect* daughter. Guilt, shame, depression all contributed to a complex eating disorder, which resulted in her coming into the hospital with considerable frequency. Suzanne knew Madison's story, but Madison struggled to talk about it in group.

Grace's eating disorder appeared rooted in a love relationship which ended horribly and a very strained relationship with her mother while growing up. She took control of her life as a high school teacher but gambled and became both anorexic and bulimic. A perfectionist in outward appearances, she struggled to find herself inside and beyond the relationship she'd built with her fiancé.

More than one mother-daughter relationship was bogged down with eating disorder triggers. I concluded one mother experienced her own issue with food because she limited her daughter's food intake to soups, like cabbage soup. She wanted to help her maintain a thinness which she, the mother, found attractive in herself. The daughter sat in process beneath a blanket. She was always cold and as thin as an Auschwitz survivor.

If insurance allowed patients to continue in the program, trust in one another grew. But, building trust took time and there wasn't always enough time because of the quick turnover.

During an education hour one day we learned the mortality rate for eating disorders was high, actually the highest of any mental illness. Suicide was all too common among individuals with anorexia and bulimia. One in five anorexia deaths was by suicide. The disease controlled the mind; the patient didn't control the disease. Fear took hold and prevented recovery in countless cases.

Relapse, recovery, death. The path followed by the individual began when the hospital door locked. The path chosen depended upon the ability to surrender control and accept the offered support.

Privacy laws prevented any follow up with patients. Where did they go? Which path did they follow? I never knew, for certain. All I did know was that I wasn't alone living with anorexia nervosa.

When asked repeatedly, in different contexts and at different times over several decades since my outpatient treatment, why I restricted what I ate, the answer rested on *fear*. Fear of gaining weight. It was an irrational but real fear. When I was growing up, my father made it clear he didn't want me, my sister, or our mother to ever become fat. When he was growing up, his mother hd been overweight, and he'd been embarrassed by that.

This statement articulated many times over the years buried itself deep inside my brain. When I began to lose weight in law school and then after my sister died, I feared a loss of control if I ate too much and couldn't stop gaining the weight back. As my parents' only surviving child, I wouldn't risk disappointing my dad by eating and getting fat, so I chose to remain thin by restricting.

I believed I couldn't control anything in life except what I put into my mouth. I was desperate to maintain control over something, so my fear would disappear. But I could never get my weight low enough for the fear to dissipate. I'd lose weight then determine nothing bad had happened, so I'd lose another pound. The cycle went on and on, until I checked into the eating disorder program.

Recovery remained elusive for most everyone at the hospital. We learned coping skills, gained weigh temporarily to stabilize, but, all too often, recovery simply wasn't achieved.

After months of learning about tools for recovery, my weight stabilized at the hospital. I was discharged as an outpatient, though I continued to drink Ensures daily, just not Ensure Plus. The ultimate motivation to survive, to move forward, came with the birth of a grandson. That motivation was sustained by the births of ten additional grandchildren. They forced me to choose. And, while relapses occur, I chose life over death from anorexia.

CHAPTER

14

SISTER'S SHADOW

Diabetes guided her food choices
but she died at thirty when I was twenty-four;
I ignored pangs of hunger
emotions tempered my food intake
of pies, pastries, pastas, and pancakes;
I discovered solace through restrictions
of quantities and entire meals.
But, restrictions, like unstoppable lava entombing Pompeii,
smothered feelings of anger, sadness, and fear,
restrictions buried unmet emotional needs.
Beneath a hardened crust of darkness,
where skeletal bones remained,
recovery was derailed.

CHAPTER

15

UNRESOLVED ENDINGS

Final exit
through unlocked hospital door,
my heart races
I trip over an untied shoelace.
Is release a mistake?
Is the scale accurate?
I look over my shoulder
wave to the girls as the door closes,
physical and emotional needs retreat
like turtles' retracted heads.
In therapy I don't feel
like anorexia is an anomaly,
but a door cuts me off,
contact's discouraged upon discharge;
we'll never learn who recovers, relapses
or dies from the eating disorders.

Aline Mohr is a poet who participated in writers' workshops, roundtables and classes after practicing law in Wisconsin. She currently resides in Charlotte, North Carolina, where she continues to write poetry and memoir.

www.ingramcontent.com/pod-product-compliance
Lightning Source LLC
LaVergne TN
LVHW011536110826
845483LV00006B/112